My Brother's Keeper

By Trey Elias Petterson
Illustrated by Eiler Brennan Pitt

We respect and honour Aboriginal and Torres Strait Islander Elders past, present and future. We acknowledge the stories, traditions and living cultures of Aboriginal and Torres Strait Islander peoples on this land and commit to building a brighter future together.

Library For All Ltd.

For so long I was so lonely.

My house was home but was not homely.

I would go to school to see my friends.

But the school bell rang, and the fun would end.

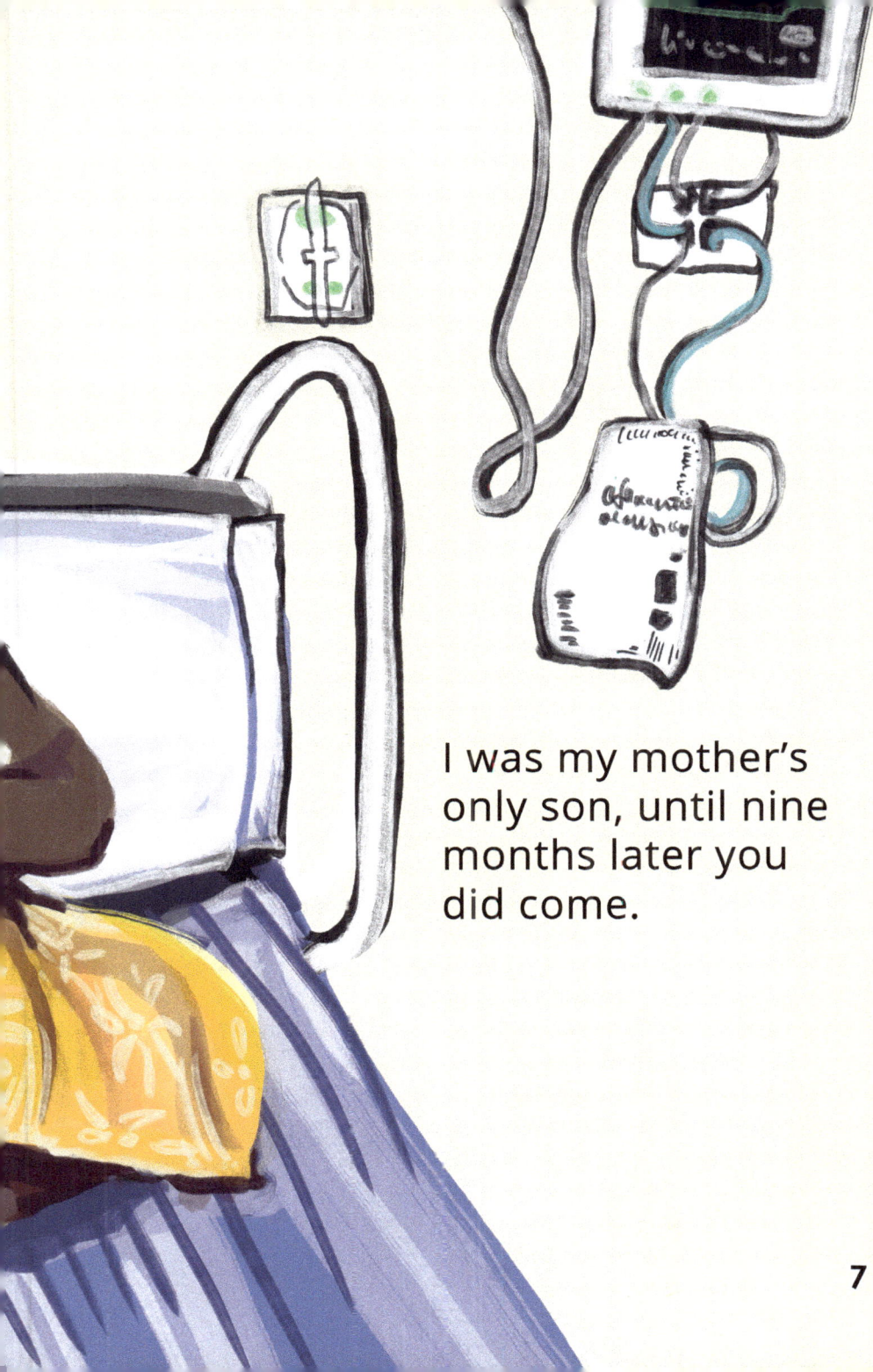

I was my mother's
only son, until nine
months later you
did come.

My new best friend.
My other half.

We would play and fight, cry and laugh.

In the morning bright, we'd race the sun.

Two hearts as one, our adventures begun.

In the cool crisp breeze, we'd chase the sky.

Our dreams as wings, we'd learn to fly.

We'd make up stories of lands so grand.

Where magic grew from the power of our hand.

We'd build our castles high and strong.

And sing sweet songs all day long.

In the night's soft glow, beneath the stars, we'd whisper secrets, show our scars.

For although we're different as night and day, together we'd find our own special way.

So hand in hand, we'd face each test.

In each other's heads, we've found our rest.

Through the highs and lows.

The journey's long.

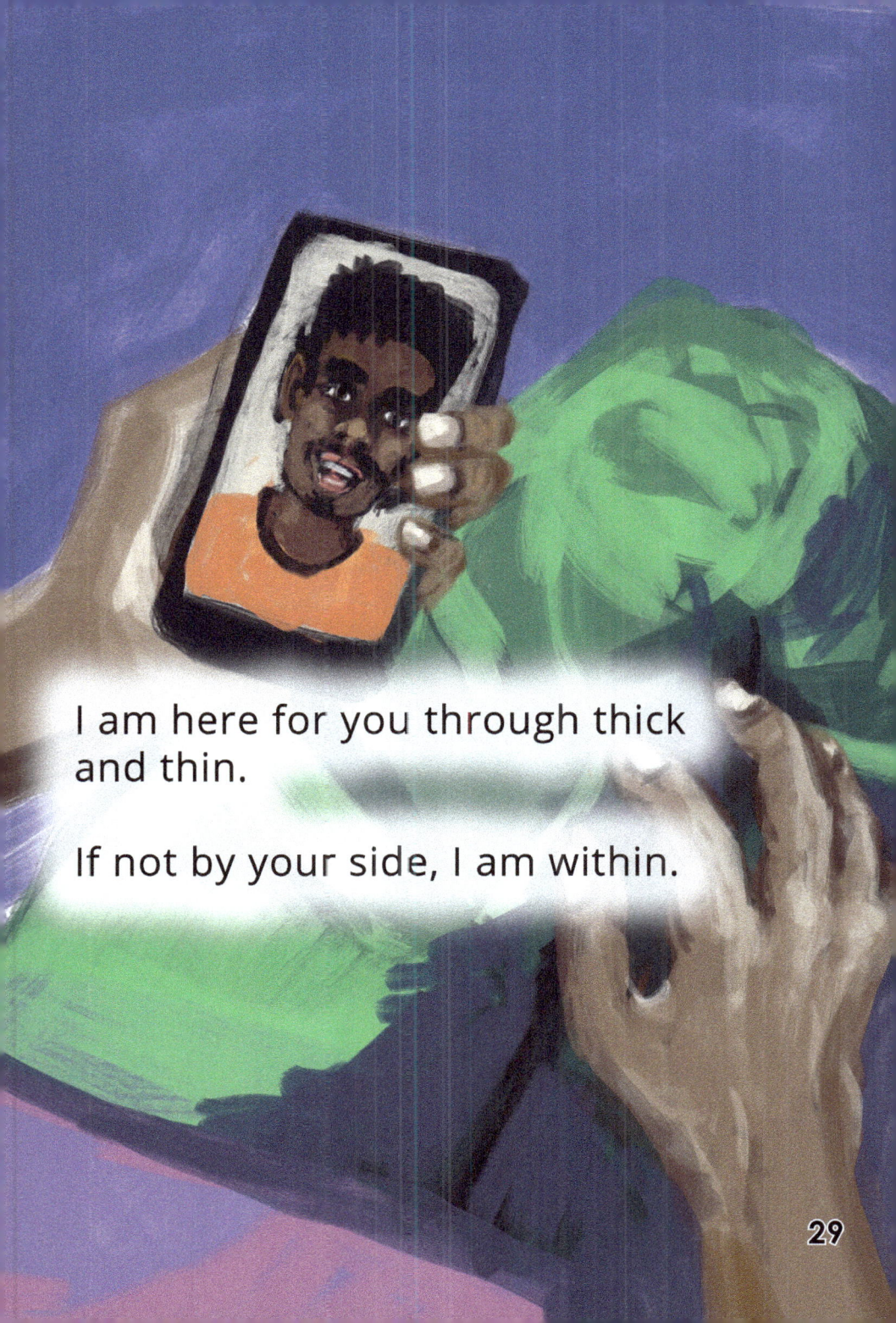

I am here for you through thick and thin.

If not by your side, I am within.

Cause life can get tough, I know this is so.

But these lifelong lessons will help you grow.

I am your keeper, and you are mine.

I love you my brother, forever in time.

You can use these questions to talk about this book with your family, friends and teachers.

What did you learn from this book?

Describe this book in one word. Funny? Scary? Colourful? Interesting?

How did this book make you feel when you finished reading it?

What was your favourite part of this book?

Download the Library For All Reader app from libraryforall.org

About the author

Trey Elias Petterson was born in Darwin on Larrakia Country. He loves fishing and playing games with his family. His favourite books as a child were *Wombat Stew* and *Possum Magic*.

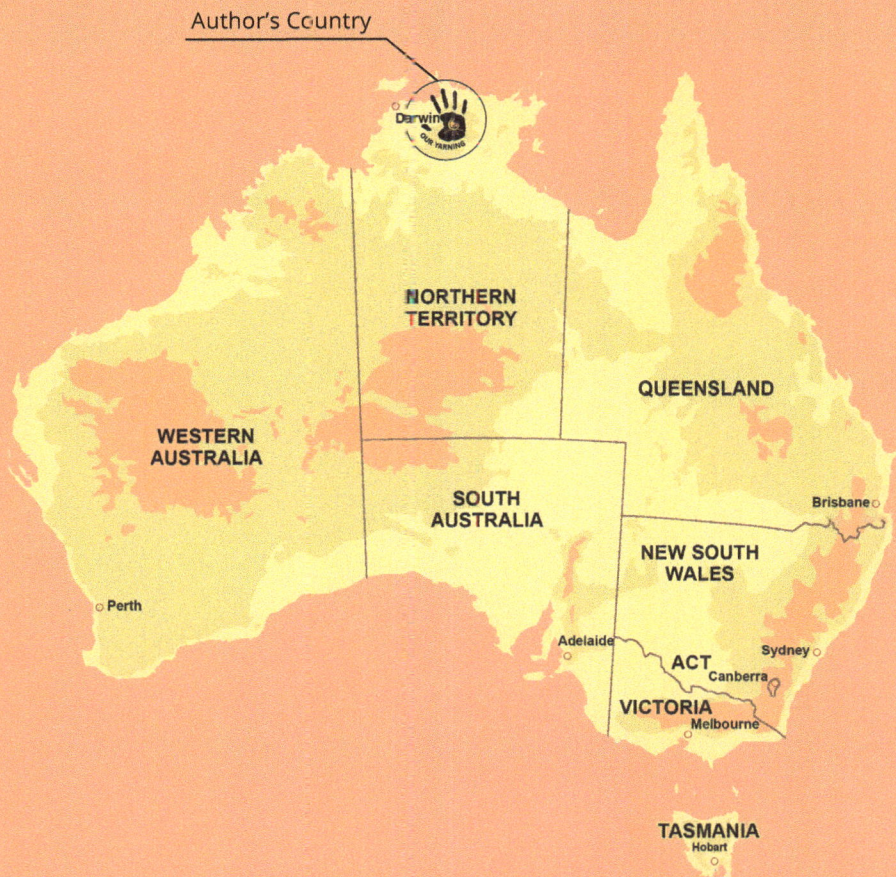

Author's Country

Darwin

NORTHERN TERRITORY

QUEENSLAND

WESTERN AUSTRALIA

SOUTH AUSTRALIA

NEW SOUTH WALES

Perth

Brisbane

Adelaide

ACT
Canberra

Sydney

VICTORIA

Melbourne

TASMANIA
Hobart

Our Yarning

The Our Yarning collection aligns with the Australian Curriculum through the Cross-Curriculum Priorities — Aboriginal and Torres Strait Islander Histories and Cultures. The collection provides an authentic opportunity for learning and embedding Aboriginal and Torres Strait Islander perspectives because it is written by Aboriginal and Torres Strait Islander people.

We know that children learn better, and enjoy reading more, when they see themselves in the stories, characters and illustrations of the books they read.

To download the app, visit the Google Play Store or Apple Store and search 'Our Yarning'.

libraryforall.org

You're reading Level 4

Learner – Beginner readers

Start your reading journey with short words,
big ideas and plenty of pictures.

Level 1 – Rising readers

Raise your reading level with more words,
simple sentences and exciting images.

Level 2 – Eager readers

Enjoy your reading time with familiar words,
but complex sentences.

Level 3 – Progressing readers

Develop your reading skills with creative stories
and some challenging vocabulary.

Level 4 – Fluent readers

Step up your reading skills with playful narratives,
new words and fun facts.

Middle Primary – Curious readers

Discover your world through science and stories.

Upper Primary – Adventurous readers

Explore your world through science and stories.

My Brother's Keeper

First published 2025

Published by Library For All Ltd
Email: info@libraryforall.org
URL: libraryforall.org

This book was created in collaboration with Yalari to improve and support the educational outcomes of First Nations children in Australia. We thank Yalari for their ongoing support of the Our Yarning program.

Educating Indigenous Children

Our Yarning logo design by Jason Lee, Bidjipidji Art

Original illustrations by Eiler Brennan Pitt

My Brother's Keeper
Petterson, Trey Elias
ISBN: 978-1-923429-96-3
SKU04643

www.ingramcontent.com/pod-product-compliance
Lightning Source LLC
Chambersburg PA
CBHW042340040426
42448CB00019B/3348